Salt, Weasel, Corpse, and Other

Jeremy Springsteed

*This collection is dedicated to the ghosts that thrash
around in my dreams*

Acknowledgments-

Body In The Nest, A Ring Beneath, Dodo, first appeared in The Free Library of the Internet Void.

Labyrinth, Southward Running Shadow, Saint Kinga of Poland, first appeared in Underwood.

Pripyat Playground first appeared in Pidgeonholes.

Our Spreading first appeared in Rue Scribe.

13 Fingered Corpse first appeared in Anapest

The Acoustics of Salt first appeared in K'in

Worm and The Underground Salt Cathedral of Poland first appeared in Z Publishing

Alone, Hiding From Hawks first appeared in Pageboy

CONTENTS

Weasel

"We are in the countryside, and of course we have wild animals everywhere."

Arnaud Marsollier head of press for CERN

Body In The Nest

That which can be used to kill
can be used to dig.
A triangle head
and two jet black eyes
are burrowing.

Six inches of slender.
It wraps its spine
and snaps its jaws.
It is always ready
to defend solitude with violence.

In winter there is metamorphosis.
The white creeps from the stomach.
Soon the entire body is white.
Soon nothing is seen.
The weasel in its body.

Accelerated

To create the beginning you need heat
and speed. You need density.
You need gold.

This is the land of quarks.
This is the tube of birth.
17 miles beneath two countries.

Non-zero fields are found everywhere.
God is discovered in particle form.
There is no spin. He is his own antiparticle.

Black holes that are lab grown.
They are held here like pets.
Time is bent down a tunnel.

We put our fingers in a stream
of unknown withins.
We keep going faster.

Alone, Hiding From Hawks

He is everywhere that is not Australia.
Slinking through grass
looking for mice to bite.
He has his home range.

He will never see another like him.
He only has reproductive relationships.
He prays that it be brief.
There are voles awaiting him.

Day and night are set to the hunt.
He must feed and sleep.
He has eggs to steal.
His life is a full time job.

The sky must be constantly searched.
They hover out of sight
and then the claws.
A flight into the end.

A Ring Beneath

Before it was buried,
before the lawsuit
claiming doomsday,
before the acceleration,
wars happened above.

The bodies fill it.
Particles fling through bullet holes.
The armies march
ever quicker
in opposing directions.

New desires raise new impact.
The enemy is always there
but he's always changing clothes.
Nemesis must be met.
There are recordable results.

Small animals live above
hunting and hiding.
Digging into time.
Their bones vibrate.
Their teeth are war.

Three Years

A lifespan that holds mystic numbers.
A trinity of years that can destroy time.
Most of their moments alone with the world.

The solitary weasel is a meditation.
"I'm here to fuck and destroy time-
we're almost out of time."

The tunnels will be pawed.
Aversions will be made.
They are those that split time.

Look at what can happen in three-
entire wars, less than presidents,
degrees, less than degrees, a takeover.

This is three-
body- mind-magic
and three

is half of six
and six is a slink
that sends us all to other.

An entire life has to be stuffed here.
How to be more is stuffed here.
Can anything double time?

Three Meters

The beast becomes man-
becomes god- becomes the bringer of death-
ends in the teeth of a beast.

This is longer than a second.
This is more than a singular collision.
This is speed and breaking.

Pulse the particle.
Push the light.
Live the black hole.

Here we have the movement-
here an honesty of not-
this is research.

We sit at the edge.
We go faster for further.
We weasel for future.

This is the acceleration
that explodes understanding.
Knowledge in unbelievable energy.

Saut du Doubs

In June a river wanders down itself.
A fall is a trickle and accessible.
There is something coming from Mouthe.
A whitening of fur is coming from the sky.

Doubs is farmed
and damned.
People always mining for power.
She only has a year to have a baby.

With a nest next to a border
she can hold her territory.
Fat on vole and ready for something.
She will tolerate trespassers.

The river will explode
50 times its mass and speed.
A fall becomes a pounding death.
Violence is taught.

She is hunger. She is the hunter.
These jaws are crushing.
She is nearing the end of her life
but now she wants babies.

She will have her kittens.
Inspect each of them.
She will feed from her body.
She will send them all away.

Amber and Teal

A tunnel that pops in blue and orange.
Teal the pipe. Amber the light.
The hidden opens in color balance.

Green wheels appear everywhere.
There are valves that hold time.
Populated with people and clipboards.

There is concert and metal
protecting the space
from earth.

See the iron yolk?
View the vacuum vessel.
This is the thermal shield!

The sound of liquid helium
is a river rushing over a fall.
Love is the heat-exchanger pipe.

In the primary experimental zone
time is twisted- or made- or broken.
The question is are there answers.

The system of accelerators
with their beams of minimum material
hold neutron time of flight.

If people build a portal to another
we are always going to build aesthetically.
Blue is time one. Orange is two.

The Meeting

A single heartbeat in all of time,
a single hunger for everything,
a single hunter that doesn't know its power.

An ununderstood instrument,
an underground loop,
an unknown becoming known.

There are two weasels.
There they sit across two times.
They're nothing but hunger.

She begins to burrow.
She begins to chew.
She begins to find a new world.

It pushes forces.
It pushes questions.
It pushes to the brink.

He keeps his hunt.
He keeps his dig.
He keeps changing time.

Only three can explain.
Only three has power.
Only three holds both worlds.

She has jumped to him.
She has bitten off too much.
She has birthed an entire new world.

It is broken.
It is no longer housing black holes.
It is birthing new realities.

He is proof of a different place.
He is proof that needs are dangerous.
He is proof and there is no ground.

If there was something solid it isn't now.
If there were lines they have been crossed.
If there was hunger it was over filled.

Over filled he leans into new.
Overfilled he slinkies for food.
Overfilled is all he knows.

No ground is safe for it.
No ground can keep a dig away.
No ground will be able to keep time.

Black holes filled her after the bite.
Black holes tried to match her eyes.
Black holes were her kittens.

Both worlds for a time have both weasels.
Both worlds have the same collider.
Both worlds are in touch with enough energy.

His hunt is a scream.
His hunt eats vole across the timelines.
His hunt will only last 3 years.

The brink of time was being tested.
The brink was pressing near the speed of light.
The brink of hunger got it chewed.

To chew was to chew.
To chew she knew would keep her life.
To chew and not care about time.

Two weasels meet in a changing.
Two weasels tolerate each other.
Two weasels disappear into each other's worlds.
Becoming known he waves goodbye.
Becoming known he gnaws away.
Becoming known he is ready to live a new world.

Its power was in speed.
Its power wasn't ready for jaws.
Its power unleashed something that only weasels understand.

The world has just changed through her.
The world is a beating heart in her mouth.
The world is digested in this.

Salt

"Here was the whole story in a picture- the message that the salt would run in damp weather was made beautifully evident."
Sterling Morton

Labyrinth

There are no minotaurs here.
The tunnel drops a quarter mile.
A plumage of salt in the earth
opens mythically downward.

Spiraling 178 miles long.
There are churches
and saints being born.
The cave is full of beseechment.

An expanse that held evil-
that has been filled
with seven centuries of corpses.
Every one perfectly preserved.

A shrine to Delphi.
A place to place our terror.
A maze of amazement.
The excavated on our table.

Today tourists walk its turns.
It is safe to reflect on horror.
Appropriate to say prayers to a princess.
Marvel at how the gray salt becomes clear.

Beyond the organized tour
the history still rages.
The mine calls to a missing Minotaur.
The salt goes uncollected.

The Underground Salt Cathedral of Poland

Between acid and base is worship.
The salt of divinity.
An atonement of NaCl.

The saints carved from miles of crystal.
The collection of pure faithful tears.
These are pious pillars.

The lord is beneath the earth.
Green on the universal indicator.
Salt is balance.

Wrapped in sodium
there is a peace of preservation.
There are various types of dead underground.

Here is the touch before art.
Here is the breath of the ocean
breathing life into people.

Here is the equal substance
that we eat
like eucharist. Here is life.

God so loved us
that he sent the largest
salty tear to dig around in.

Mouth of Moloch

The fire king swallows offerings.
His heated chamber demands everything.
He is a gateway but first the flame.
He is a chasm. People slide down his throat.
They chip at his salty teeth.
Horns piping out the ash of children.

In the 13th century he began to open his mouth again.
For 700 years he devoured and was devoured.
Nazis hide among his molars.
He is a hungry god. He calls out-
"Justice is in my stomach!"
and people go running like Canaanites.

If a salt mine were a whale
people would become willing Jonahs.
Sitting in its salty belly
praising a god that could hold us
nearly womb like. A life sacrificed
to a paradise of gut.

Moloch distributed worldwide.
Moloch in everything. He is of the earth.
Wars around his teeth. He is a feast.
Licking the walls of his mouth.
Moloch we taste you
before we finally enter you.

Saint Kinga of Poland

Before they came to take her from her home
she cast the burdened engagement ring
into the Maramures salt mine.

This is a time of miracles and arranged marriages.
Her wedding ordained and necessary.
An affair filled with chastity.

Along ribbons of salt
the ring travels to Wieliczka.
A miner breaks it free from a crystal.

A sign that you would die trying to forget.
This was the beginning of your ascension.
A title of princess to be rejected.

A saint will rise from this salt.
She towers 331 feet underground.
She holds charity for even those beneath the earth.

700 years after her death
she was brought to the hall of the saints.
Her name continues to change.

The Acoustics of Salt

For Zbigniew Preisner

As I read Corinthians 13;
thinking of marriage and Europe,
divorce;
holding myself through nightmare,
fighting a sheet of shame-
I am forced to sit in your empty spaces.

You rise like a sea-
imperceptible until too late.
You fill sanctuary with warbling hope.
You sing the final century of a mine.
You know the vibration of salt.
You are commissioned to sit in the pit.

The assembly is held in Wieliczka.
Here you will tell the story
of the nightmare of the rising
and the falling
of humanity in the 20th century.
Here your acoustics will be perfect.

History and philosophy
are who taught you notes.
So many say learn from math
but you say what about Job.
You are a secret garden
that tunnels my ear to make me feel.

In the cave that your people built
and the Germans tried to kill you from
(before you were born you were born to war)
your song was lifted to the sky.
The weight of rebirth in every note.
We are the salt of the earth.

Uncommon Lake

When found we are usually found without salt.
We are found to be pure and a manifestation
of the mystery of an unknowable planet.

A world that seems to want people on it.
A place that demands worship or death.
A water based civility.

Yet here I sit in the base of a salt mine.
The salinity is not from me.
This is my home beneath the earth.

A lake in a crystal.
A pathway for a ring to travel
from Hungary to a sainted Poland.

As a lake I am unaware
of my actual saltiness.
I'm just a subterranean lake.

I imagine-
if lakes are allowed to imagine-
that I am still in the house of refreshing.

I am that which adorns chappals.
The important note that reads-
HOLY!

House of Crystal

The workers are at home in work.
A callous for a bed.
They carve out their own comfort.
This labor is life.

This work- the corner of every meal.
Even the loaves require this.
Work is a body
that they break.

Look and see the power of work.
Across time and war and flood
they pull their bodies from the mine.
These are the homes that live in hands.

The morning march is an anthem-
Here I go turning life into gold,
here I pickax my way to death,
here I go expelling power.

In their sleep
the chasm enters their dreams.
So committed to a task
that near death has no power.

They haunt these shafts and hallways-
still scraping walls for families long dead.
A measurable work is never undone.
Underground everything is alive.

Flame Clarity

Heat allows a passage of light.
Things have to be rearranged
to allow illumination in gray salt.

The crystal tells us there is more.
It is saints and chandeliers,
it is myth and faith.

Within the melt there is newness.
A breakdown isn't loss
it is reconstruction.

Nearly 200 miles of statuary.
A temple waiting to be purified.
A world site.

The workers took their hands
to the task of remember.
Carving forever across this cave.

The salt is always clear
if it has been tempered right-
however, it is the same salt.

Corpse

"We were at once recipients of and contributors to the joy of witnessing the sudden appearance of creatures none of us had foreseen, but which we ourselves had nonetheless created."

Simone Kahn

Unnamed Corpse

miasma feminine trespass evenly
(liar forthcoming
(pry your cold hands(
what cannot comes knocking nightly
(artist provides what life can't(
après moi le déluge(
right into the blue frog's mouth
(forsakenly cravenly restless
(after that lily pad sky(
face warm echochamber(
confessions make wings
(birds don't need
(but confusion still floats lungs(
accord the wheezing rusted men)

Take Years You Said

it must for mold to set)
only hours for film to form)
across the shower)
the water makes real into image)
to real image)
don't let the drain occupy)
made for gravity and liquid tension
) everything disposable
) sharp blades)
a flip of a switch)
whirrrr)
were things to remain
) for you to deal with
) pens   cups   grandfather's dentures
) a bite out of time)
eat the face of the wrist
) suck the narrows)
narrate nature
) angle meaning
) time made for you
) make some time)

Fermentation Of A Fern As Seen From A Text Message

A fern unfurled from her forehead-
fiddlehead galaxy spiraling.

That you Jeremy,
a nature poem
urging lines about slugs?

Left mucous stained tracks
when it tried to let go.
Unseasonably winter.
Premature unicorn.

Her forehead was a block of muck Swiss
through hair moss-
matted and slick,
no blossom,
no seed.

Into soil her fingers earth like roots.
Fonds like ratios extended-
they only know nautilus warning,
they only know arsenic,
the smell of root rot.

Drink poison,
learn not to see
in the dark
rising from the cellar.

Drunk Dog

You always were the hair of the dog
Since you left I've become infatuated
Can't click crumb because cackle pause
With collar bones and left fingers
The lay of the land the time of the day

A leftover of last night
You were the hair stuck in the back
A delusion of like-heals-like
When I kiss I part my lips
That gin soaked smile

The rock of the lake effect even
Drenched in kerosene and cinnamon
My throat the rock in David's pocket

In the morning of your fallout
Over them it is almost enough
Pulling cat hair from your overcoat
I collect fur and try to remember
I get out of bed every morning
When you look at me you only see reflection
My mouth always fills with blood

Itch Wrenching Corpse Unsolvable

feeling less finite
(find a verb and slap it in(
swim bladder with wingtips stretched
(here where wind won't let lilacs bloom(
some god shark tale splits
(I took flight swim and stock
(with a cargo of lamps(
I was in a wing of the state(
greater than(
water   sunshine   cathedral
(begotten by holy I don't believe in(
surface separations gave me these hands
(unsolvable(
feet this hair
(fresh as a thing jaded by limpid colors
(but recently begun in unsightly depths(
several savage artisans mother ocean
(to blood tearing feather(
though finless(
not breathless(
and though itch retching
(is simple)

In The Middle; a Candle

stick the wick in your sleep
(eye drips warm candles over my paper plate
(the palm of my hand a river black with nowhere
) sleep into Thursday dream(
out by the closing eyelid
(while Stellar Jay and blind puppeteers trip on)
the candle of the eye drips cold(
from a girl searching for wicks
(light it and alchemy with no end
) while I click through a flame(
warmth like each channel(
sunrise always barfs up TV dinners
(a lifetime of return)

13 Fingered Corpse

Typewriter bruised but not beaten.
She wonders why he couldn't see,
digging deeper yields dark wells.

The letter buried under her fingernail was Q.
Never thought of Q until it was missing.
It stands for quail when I think of you.

The letter creviced between her nostrils was an Armenian loan-
the first initial of her first lover,
he whisked her vessel off to face threats unknown.

She searched fractal soil for the U.
You were tucked behind her teeth-
frayed bits of reed   tip from Dali's ear.

It was unhidden   unlocked aperture of mouth.
World from behind her eyes held too many secrets,
soup spelling out barcodes.

Quaint cuticles bleed alphabet,
lurks benevolent mind scanning,
cosmic bridge in his mischief.

I'd rolled an O before,
giving it crutch it seemed
it needed.

Where Bats Go When They Go Wrong

When the echolocation gets fishing boat jammed
the whole colony plunges moth happy to the ocean floor.

I'll make your moth happy
if you know what I mean.

Black bodied moth
not burnt to the flame, no
shard edges to ignite
but to blend
to ward off predators
to symbolize pollutants
clinging to the trees.

When she screams my feet race to the kitchen
when I get there
the sink has already overflowed.

It's okay- I'll hold the door.

The water's response to the offering-
dolphins take cloud residence.

Corpse In A Frog's Mouth

The sky is leaking.
Stars streaking forked tongues.
A box full of Jupiter's lies.

Each of these will collapse,
an obsolete constellation
passes over the hills.

Birth is a carbon backbone.
As the tongue furls
like dandelions.

Each bud fills with carbon.
They yacht away.
Wings crystallize; we inhale.

At the end of collapsing stars' life;
a black hole.
The powder from the insect's body.

See nothing unusual.
From here at the at the width of it
I find no name.

Only the glow that pushes lids.
Pupils inhaling.
I cannot count the number of times.

I told you to stop looking at me.
Taste your saliva.
Smell snakes on the dormant heaven gate.

The fryer knows not flesh nor wing
of them yet still consumes crackles.
At the end of the frog's tongue

a moth.
The dust
a spiral of stars,

a parade of anti matter in flux
with canvas.
This palette of a song.

The tunnel's melody plays on.

Corpse Could Embrace Ideological Ingenuity

piston as piston becomes foreign
(wanting to remember
to sweet forget
(to build structures of sweat filled September
) chords sickening melody
(tooth rotten(
see the systems take hold(
you turn and turn
) innocent you contribute(
wanting clean to mean more
(not just rinsed because mold can be)
sweet cheese is rot(
rot telling that cheese is proof(
contamination sustained us)
decomposition is proof of love(
sugars consumed in chemistry
(to be held
) mildew smells smelled)

Hummingbird Corpse

In the city one never sees
(a dead hummingbird crawling
(but a live one
(in pursuit of their heart(beats too loudly
(wings flutter too quick)
We see dead photographer
(gnawed knuckle(
eyeballs done and missing(
but birds)
There are dead Hummers
(burnt out aside the road
(like Afghan corpses
(to hide the crash(
into dark to hide
(the broken feathers we pass(on the birdless street)

Other

"But precisely because I exist by means of the Other's freedom, I have no security;
I am in danger in this freedom."

Jean-Paul Sartre

Cacophony For Four Voices

All the witches free
And then they blow

Apart like leaves

Yesterday was electric

And dead

I can't I can't

Bats of my friends

Dusk in the dumpster

Remember sky smolder
I was a teenage werewolf

I dress myself in blood
Floating above blocks

Concert is conspiring
Listen

Your hair is everywhere

The smell of oncoming

The burn of the march

Now we bow our heads

The smell of oncoming
The burn of the march

Now we bow our heads

Palms like offense

Like raptured silence

I can't I can't

Everything is a body

Every ear broken

We are digging in infection
Once there were grandparents

There were trips to the dump
Mud invades memory

They keep sweeping
Cat eyes in their belly buttons

All the witches free

All the witches free

And then they blow

Apart like leaves

All the witches free
Cat eyes in their belly buttons

They keep sweep-
ing

These days until tomorrow

Mud   invades memory

There were trips to the dump

There were once grandparents

We are digging in infection

Every ear is broken
Everything is a body

I can't I can't
Like raptured si-lence

Palms like offense
Now we bow our heads

The burn of the march

The smell of on-coming

Your hair is every-where
Listen

Palms like offense

Like raptured silence

I can't I can't

Everything is a body

Every ear is broken

We are digging in infection

Once there were
grandparents
There were trips to the
dump
Mud invades memory
These days until tomorrow
They keep sweeping

Cat eyes in their belly
buttons
All the witches free

Yesterday was electric

And dead

I can't I can't

Bats of my friends

Dusk in the dumpster

Remember the sky smolder

I was a teenage werewolf

I dress myself in blood

Floating above blocks
Laughter on the street
Concert is conspiring

Listen

Your hair is everywhere

Concert is con-
spiring
Laughter on the
street
Floating above
blocks
I dress myself in
blood
I was a teenage
werewolf
Remember the sky
smolder
Dusk in the
dumpster
Bats of my friends

I can't I can't
And dead
Yesterday was
electric
Apart like leaves

All the witches free

Haunting

Cementing the carpet with my blood.
Bubbles as my bloodless brain fumes.
Oil sheen night. The wind purple and blue.

The world glides over itself. There was a bird.
Then I'm being shook awake
and juice is served and separations to attain.

Turning a corner in sleep
I come to face
that bird. It stalks my forms.
Tail promising maps to paradise.

The shape of a bee eater.
The size of an eagle. The colors burn eyes.
Flames for wings with moss and ice center.

It says nothing but is there awareness.
Monogamous, it has chosen me.
Loves me in possibility.

Entire days spent in plumage and why.
Trying to ignore signs as they slap.
I keep meeting dead birds and dreaming impossible ones.

Scouring poems and ornithological texts.
No drawing of primary wing can provide answer.
Nightly enveloped in feathers. Winging to each morning.

Dodo

I negate the day.
Cut myself out of the world
and do the work of defining that
which is this removed portion.

To speak of invasive species-
brought across climates
by accident or as gift
to remind a loved one of home.
Nothing in the new environment
recognizes this plant.
The ivy engulfs a hill.
It only takes one creeping vine.

Phenotypic plasticity-
the ability of a living thing
to change its physical attributes
to become better suited.
Some plants may grow a deeper tap root
to suck more nutrients
or some unfurl broader leaves
to consume more sun.

An enlarging self.
Creeping positive displacing negative.

Predatory plants-
birds drop the strangler fig
seeds on top of canopy.

Growth begins at the branch level,
roots growing down.
Often killing the host.
Leaving a hollow tree,
pure exterior.

Dusty descends the dodo
from the grips of extinction
to stand as the moments double symbol-
dead and dumb.

See the large land dove,
thick beaked no natural predators.
Ill suited to anywhere but its isolated island.
Comes man
with an onslaught of
dogs, pigs, cats.
The nests that litter the ground
easy prey for a prodding tusk.

So easy for people to hunt,
though they tasted terrible.

Within 100 years of their brush with western men
the last dumb dodo dies.

This pain-
the expulsion of everything that is not self.
I creep out into my negative.

A diminishing me allows
the world its perfection.
Only my eye

and words
tell me otherwise.

I want to live in the world of my negatives.
Push the inside out.
The bone to hold the skin safe.

I want to eradicate these borders.
This flesh of location.
When the empty space part in an atom in my hand
touches another atom's empty space.
What is touching the limits?

What identity isn't violence?
A ripping away from all that is not it.
What is this false unity that holds me whole?
Who could be singular in this flow of energy and time?

Southward Running Shadow

1

Because the sky keeps turning to ash
we walk drained to the smoking area.
I dust the cafe several times a day
but the destruction still accumulates.

What else to do
as the storm drives down
to where my daughter lives?

The threat that my grandfather fought
were one half of a battle.
The flag that he was buried with
returned and joined those who he fought.
He didn't win a war.

I haven't slept in a garage in months.
The police are seizing the fray.
Each day becomes more volcanic.

I await a tide.
I drag a beach fire to the challenge.
I dare someone to stop this.

We hold mobs of compassion.
We ram ash covered arms into hope.
We flood with correct now.
We faith in forward.

2

An apogee 750 miles high.
It hangs eclipse between earth and moon.
It is a stitch, out and back in.

The five minute thrust,
a cut from gravity. A needle
to space. The totality of return.

Tests are executed. Results feared.
My friend lives in the local blast zones.
Back at home we're too busy drowning to help.

It keeps getting hotter here.
In the west we've been smoke training.
Some of us will have to live.

I've been saying plague prayers over flames.
I'm calling locust. I'm calling jellyfish.
The toads turn to blood so everyone calms down.

We sit together with the threat
of a vaporization stitch work.
These needles are pointed everywhere.

Traveling for two minutes at four miles a second,
the target is quick,
I hope to be in the inner cloud.

A horror of promise of peace.
For once we'll be all together
watching the air turn to fire.

3

Topping the tank.
He's driving from Ohio.
An event within a series of events.

The pathway curves south.
There are collisions and obscuring figures.
A fester of finality.

These dead things
pulled from the ground, refined,
they require us to place something in return.

The man of soldiering age
goes soulless to battle.
His intention is to sackcloth the sun.

Excitement as a hot coal in the throat.
There will be a crossing in space.
People prepare for a momentary mass migration.

An event within a series of events.
Although it is well mapped
there are still eclipse deniers.

Outside the totality zone cites stop.
All citizens gaze up through dark lenses.
These are the events that stop wars.

A burning for totality
with the secret faith
that the darkness is transformation.

Driving headlong into 10:20 am PST,
there is eerie everywhere.
A questioning of light the rest of the day.

Within the chain of events
comes the promise of an invigoration
of a collision that longs to last a score.

These are the new mechanics.
No longer a slide by. No momentary shadow.
These pistons beat into other pistons.

The engines froth.
The exhaust sneers.
The moon accelerates.

In the desert last night
a city became a battleground.
The friction becoming flame.

We know not to look at the naked sun.
An event within an event.
We're still waiting for the shadow to pass.

4

The summer was stabbed open
on a light rail train in Portland.
The warmth drawing a pale spectacle from the ground.
The year started with a gun shot in Red Square.

They are showing up everywhere.
They're in cars. They're in hats.

They hold office and the ears of officers.
They're carrying pepper spray and shields.

A plague of drunken rats.
The stink of sun warmed shit.
They gnaw my eyes while I sleep.
They hide in plain sight during the day.

The herald demons who sing end.
Desperate, they don't think
that the sky has enough smoke in it.
They go hunting through hurricanes.

"Salvation through extinction,"
shouted from a car
 barreling towards a mass of people.

5

These final gifts
from the summer rage
before it passes to a vengeful fall.
Birthed from winter violence
and the despair of spring.

The right eye passed over Texas
bringing a litter of explosions.
Water is evil in this arrangement.

The left eye is looking for Florida.
It sees to everything.
The wind tells false psalms.

The flaming tongue that is Montana.
Our homes are burning or drowning.
We live on a long on fire in the ocean.

Storms keep birthing in the sea.
When will one pass over
my daughter in Virginia?

The rumors of fall are everywhere.
No one can tell what it will exact.
These are the days of broken records.

In cafes and bars there is acceptance
that the conclusion is coming.
The conversation isn't even whispered.

Worm

I watched a worm, rain drummed from
the dirt, work
to the edge of the curb.
One could say
this is about perseverance but today
value of futility.

I had no hope but stayed watching.
Chugging whole body.
Slinking into gutter with last year's
leaves. Swaying for
safety. Pulsating further onto the asphalt.
Every part of

its squish in peril. Those are risks
born into a worm.
There needs no purpose. The worm is
crossing the road.
Knowing only eviction and suffering forward.
Expanse of road

eternal. All is understood as struggle.
An other side.
Faith. There is no sun, no
snakes. Worm has
never encountered grass. Desire is not
available in its economy.

Wriggle and rigor are the same.
Blocks smashed smear

of struggle. But worms keep living.
I hardly breathe.
Digging comfort from insects and raccoons.
Then the traffic

flattens those standing in its way.
I could have
watched the struggle all day but
a city demands.
I thought of the worm for hours
and sign wondered.

But a worm not in sight
is very silent.
I watched and then was haunted
by a worm
inching carelessly into a hopeless situation.
We make due

with what is available. To be
honestly boneless. What
unavailable hiding places would open up?
To be meaningless
yet compelling. The work of shadow
but still believed.

Nothing will change. No magic cocoon.
No beautiful transformation.
I watched and studied and left
it to tangle around.
To be pointlessly boneless. Cluelessly free.
Charge across darkness.

Hunger of depth and cooler blindness.
Dreams of loam.
Nothing depends on the worm's calling.
Unseen with peril.
No I but that I gave.
Always to further.

Explanation of My Maniac Hair

Under my scalp lives a colony of ants.
Above each thorax is tied a hair.
The strands are attached to gearworks.

They turn a tune in the twin music boxes of my eyes,
inside the boxes are ballerinas,
they stand on glass orbs
with their crowned heads facing into the center of my head
the orbs are filled with moths.

They thrash themselves against the aperture of my pupil.
The inside of my skull is filled with fried eggs.
Inside the yolks are the bodies of the recently dead
that I used to clean as a twenty year old.

My cheekbones are formed from every lie I've told my mother.
My teeth made from my daughter's dreams,
my jaw is a trigger waiting to be pulled.

As the ants work around these elements they become frantic.
Their ant hearts cannot keep up.
As they die my hair thins
exposing the outside of a geode.

When the man at the fair cuts open the stone a murder of crows
come flapping out.
They have the face of your worst ex lover
cawing like your friend who died as a child
leaving the crystalline hollow to distort the light of the sun.

Even With Fireworks

If this were the mountain west
we would stumble oven dry
through the well kept grass of SLC.
I can see you working a poem late at night
on a lawn in the Avenues.
But this is a salutary NYC July.

Peddling into a knot of people
awaiting a sky of bloom.
Crowds have become a new form of distress.
In the fear there is fun
hiding like a gun in a waistband.

This is the season of smell.
The locals flee if they can afford it.
Rightly, I am here. My face should be a warning.

Every neighborhood I show up in
reprices, reallocates, redistricts.
I am the white canary.

The bikes we ride
in a mixed pack of ties and cutoff shorts
down second avenue
as rush hour thickens.

We were lamenting the locking of the dark cube
on Lafayette. Someone wrote on the base,

"This is why this city is shitty,"
and I felt at home.

I'm the same ashy tear no matter the climate.
This is supposed to be a love poem
for a friend but the darkness of the hour
is always creeping in.

For My Birthday

The ship well on its way
when it saw a wall of storm.
Forgetting where the wind blew from.
This is the face of birth in 1980.
We meme among the albatross.
We've met you in the ice jam.
Born in decline.
Told, be grateful always.
Pledge allegiance.
Our broken is our blood.
Beat and beat but blood will find blood.
There are places that they tell
tale of man becoming god
but only if you're not marked.
We're descended from the sellouts.
A comfort built from fear.
Love built with blinders.
There was Ronnie
with his ray guns
commanding kids to follow,
then the classroom challenger.
All these plagues ago-
the stillness of indifference
is the same crossed arms
and rolling eyes.
Told to learn
but when we manage to hold a pen

or begin to cite sources; a slap and a scold.
We cry our way out of ice
only to be shot
by those that should praise us.

I Think You Are A Mirror

For: C.M.

Every time I make my trip home
I want you there,
Strange and no longer sad, almost smiling for me.

 How silly we must seem
sliding down Salt Lake streets, strolling in love
with our sickness, with each other's hand.

Oh, how we sit in loud cafes
dreaming of your world and talking,
Endlessly talking about how you hate your school
and this phrase or that idea,
of how you want kids.
Baby blue hotel night, you
and she and too much cocaine.
And she loves you but drags you
on and on with her talk of some other love affair with some
moron who doesn't even come close to you, who mathematically
proved his love for her when you
can just say it.
Leaves you in your corner pawing at the hem of her Levis that
she took off in that room
and invited you into your first.
(I think you are a mirror.)
I should have been there.

Wait for my turn
and I tell you about how for a moment
looking in a mirror in a dirty bathroom,
acid, bleeding thumb and beer.
I heard the voices of fiery angels,
they told me that I am the sun in flesh.
I tell you this statistic and that awful fact.
We laugh and embrace in the grass.

It is a dark night walk in Liberty Park,
sounds and bikes with your stories,
elicit sexual encounters with older men,
who and why they sucked your cock.

You say you want children,
little boys in little pants
who love you because of your genes.

All I say is nothing.
All I think is no;
maybe I'm a Marxist
or I know you hated your father,
I hate my father
and you are too beautiful to be hated by children,
or the bombs will be flying, let's keep the death numbers down,
anything but I think that you are too unstable,
that anyone as lost in their own mess as we
should not care for a scraped knee.

Always back to San Francisco,
our midnight exodus,
your chocolate covered snap in Sacramento,

your morning flee back to our Egypt,
our salted valley.

Yes, you order the wine.
You know far more than I who only drink beer.
Yes, oysters,
you know far more than my empty monk like belly.

Staring across the table I think it strange
that I should feel like the father.
Sick to my stomach everyday,
worried that you've gone too far,
that it is the finale swing of sane.
I who hate family
and all the warm wet feelings that go with,
I who want to end the world
(I think you are a mirror.)
would want to hold you to my chest,
coo you and say that you're alright.

I think that you are a mirror
and you scare me. When you see me
I see me and you see you
and we are locked this way love.

A Memory of A Pillar of Salt

She told me to keep my toe
above my heart.
I worried about stretching.

She asked why all the books
I read are filled with canned fish.
I stopped reading years ago.

She burnt toast
like it was an indecipherable joke.
Laughing into the smoke detector.

She bred moths
to be released in daycare centers
because she loved children.

She danced to the sound
of leaf blowers and weed wackers.
Everyone else closed their windows.

She wore clothing made of speaker wire,
a felt wig, a mask of leaves.
A breathing collage.

She stood behind me
and whispered warmly,
"Why are you following me?"

She hid oranges in the toilet,
newspapers in the dryer,
cat fur in my shoes.

She broke into
the homes of sleeping people.
Woke them and asked if they were dreaming of her.

She was an accumulation of dust.
A year's worth of dead skin cells.
She was evidence of the movement of bodies.

She called racoons her mother
and flickers father.
She was never born. She is constant return.

Baroqueluminecence

The body of the saint
based in the dust of fireflies.
True tenebrism; radical naturalism of death on death.

Caravaggio the crepuscular-
the cold light of papal death warrants.
When luciferin reacts with oxygen,

when the night is so dramatically,
pin-pointedly lit
luciferase is the speed.

But what is known of kelip-kelip,
of synchronicity of sociability,
of diet or altitude?

These last few nights
of sweaty Virginia walks
the bioluminescence like the finger of Christ

singling out Matthew.
"You brawler," it buzzes,
"as a child you glowed as a warning

but what now do your chemicals mean?"
Latreille, your heatless fever
snuffed out on your way to pardon.

The guts of a poisonous toad,
the light of angelic.
A shift with no value other than itself.

Pripyat Playground

A never opening park of culture and rest.
The chamomile paratroopers without laughter
don't make the trip to the ground.
Radioactive a week before opening.
The workers plastic wrapped inside their homes.

Conflicts that remain unresolved
because no one could bump them out
within an allotted time on the autodrome.
Ice cream unscoped. Trash cans empty.
Children that are now losing a second set of teeth.

Ants in heaps under the Russian swing.
The pendulum motionless on an expired sea.
Heat of the failure digs through the soil.

Summer vacation never comes.
The Geiger counter keeps saying no.

After 31 years the circular overview awoke.
Rotating the way Ferris wheels beg for.
Then returned to its historical position.
Like hands on a dead clock.
Forever waiting for opening day.

Chipmunk

I'm greedily myself
and hoard all this blood in my vault of skin.

Pinning everything
in the shadowbox of my mind.

I push the blade of my body
down sidewalks and through cafe doors.

Everything is cut by my glance.
I slice myself out of everything

and then go slashing things
apart with names and boundaries.

Even those that I love
aren't safe from the violence of language.

I say with force,
"I adore you

You are alone.
More so, you're alone in my aloneness."

Like a despot I go on
writing love poems

condemning the parts
that I have already slashed from the whole.

When the chipmunk stores the nut
it does so without name;

its like nothing happened at all.
The blade of me has done it's work

I have pinned down the rodent
and its cache.

Emptying My Aunt's House After Her Death In Saint George, Utah

I travel a thousand miles
across states and shocks of culture
to perform my final acts of family.

In the house once owned by the famous polygamist
that my aunt so suddenly died in.
Even the pomegranate tree is grieving in the heat.

Outside in the dry air
the hills that hold this city
are jealous of the flame of her hair.

My mother looks through the rooms
for anything that holds the shape of her sister's life.
Endless dog toys and flashlights fill her closets.

That is not where we find her.
In the park at dusk the residents of the desert
sing her powers.

The children lament their lost friend.
The dogs yip and lick
but do not see the woman who spoke their language.

A balm to almost all the crestfallen;
maybe all but herself.
I'm fearing the relapses.

I'm craving the moist of my northwest home
like I crave the embrace of her living eyes.
I could have been here in life

but I was only paying attention to my feet.
I should have been writing about her departed dog
but couldn't read the depths of despair.

All I can do is box dishes
to donate to the poor.
Even in death she is giving.

Our Spreading

We left home across ocean.
Virginia hills and bootleg routes,
hand cart Mormon pilgrims.
We move west and when there is no more west
we fall to the shore drinking ocean to expose more land.
We leave our old gods to the east in search of Zion.
When Zion is found we leave the valley in search of Shangri-la.

We are sparse like southern Idaho.
We are towering like the Wasatch front.
We are dead fly ridden Great Salt Lake.
There is no upward movement in this clan, only expansion.

Drink drug depraved dreamers.
Silent saints of salt and sky.
Poor chicken coop dwellers,
couch surfers, park campers.
Wanderlust in the veins,
dissatisfaction in the DNA.

We want to be there in our own annihilation.
We open our bodies to offer
nerve and bile
to the unfeeling and the overfilled.
Some drank or drink
or would still drink but they've gone to the ground.
Outcast aunt
drank until she had titanium pins put into her ankle
eventually lost that foot because she keep

passing out in the backyard
in the tomatoes,
the hose running everywhere.

Sometimes we wake up in Vegas
with hangover and regret and nothing
but the shirt on the back, even the car gambled away.
Successfully being demoted back to private thirteen times
for drinking, bet fixing, insubordination and still put up for promo-
tion again.
Sight big enough to take in the whole of Pocatello to Walla Walla
and never raise a potato from the earth
We marry and marry and marry again
and eventually just live with our exes
because it's cheaper rent.

The Mormon Boys of Early Autumn

First fireplaces of fall are waking up.
Smoke smells familiar
like the face of a friend lost
invading a daydream.

The Mormon boys are out hunting doors.
Two missionaries at a time, respectful hair.
They don't try to talk to me.

Their predictability is a comfort
like the return of rain.

These two are like smoke.
They conjure faces
and half remembered words.

I hear my bishop
rubbing his dry hands,
"Do you masterbate?"
All eyes trying to peer through drywall.

They're in shirts and ties;
I'm in black and furrowed brow.
They have books and pamphlets
and I have mine.

What does the drifting smoke
do to their memory?
Do they see their mothers,

or a girlfriend
that has moved on?

The odor fills me with ghosts.
The crisp of September is solitude.
The breeze shows that which was avoided.
The air was like this when I turned away,
digging towards some unnamed more.

Between the smoke and the boys
I hear myself twenty years ago
vowing to not accumulate regrets.
Look at all that I have collected.

The Dark Return

Crows swirl around my head
while far above an eagle is tossed
in the wind of an incoming storm.

Trees ungulate as the pressure changes.
Leaves the color of blood and sun
dance in chaotic convulsions.

Even in this dying season
everything is teeming with life.
Even this gray contains light.

Here we pay for the green
with dark and soak.
We pay in cracking bones.

Soon the sun takes its leave.
Soon the blankets heavy on the body.
Behold the blooming mold!

The things that get fat and sleep
are finishing their glut.
The rest of us greet the season of the night.

Thanksgiving With The Family That Took Me In

Helping a teenager write an essay.
Describing people hundreds of years dead
but using her words to do it.

We talk of tea and taxes.
We talk of thesis and support.
A wild family swirls around us
as we do the serious work.

We don't talk about my daughter.
We keep silent about the times when they were both small
and hiding in my arms,
terrified of the scene of the cartoon dog that went to hell.

In the kitchen the mothers
prepare the feast
working in a fog of laughter.
Out front uncle and little brother
kick the soccer ball around.

Sitting with Grace
I'm not full of loss.
I save my grief for home.
I'm where I should be
even if I always carry a wound.

Later there will be beer
and talk of villainy.
Later I will sit on my bed
and stare at my empty hands.

For these few hours
I'm family like the mutt I found
when I was six was family,
before I took him to school
and all the authorities
said that the dog was no kin to me
and took him away.

Pitfall

) Hands held out. Pitcher full of frogs.
) Nectar bribes disrupt direction.
) Waxy flakes that lead to digestive pit.
) A small gap releases excess.)

) Deceptive flower sits and kills.
) Mouth always open and accepting.
) Slope to dissolve so inviting.
) Even birds have been lost in the embrace.)

) Taking root in nutrient starved soil,)
this is where the dead go to thrive.)
The ants go marching down
) exhausting themselves into lunch.)

) This leaf rolling trick,
) sometimes wearing hats to keep the rain out.
) Full of deceptively sweet water.)
Rats fall in. Even fur is consumed.))

The cobra is thin.
) Light leading insects to confusion.)
There is no exit only chamber.
) Here is the dry balloon holding a million gnats.))

These beautiful traps.)
Slip into a pod)
and become part plant.)))

Snap

A single disruption won't set off the trap.
Two hairs must move to snap.
Five more bring a tightening.

When the waterwheel snatches
the lobes close in milliseconds.
Long hairs assure food not garbage is enclosed.

The midrib cells collapse and release the tension.
A trick of scent lands them on the open red)
soon to be plant stomach.

Called mouse or bear
or fly or man trap
the result of the embrace is the same.

Consuming nitrogen
the soil is void of.
How has the snap come to be

People keep Venus as a pet.
Something about the devour tells them
that it's okay to crush or be crushed.

Beach 2 La Push

A taunt to the indifference that any closer would take us.
Nest of hemp cord, heartwood, balled notebook paper.
Decorated with wood shavings.
Housed in soaked through logs.

We've come defiant. Here to pillage and burn.
Face flat on the sand stoking flame. Zero foot elevation.
Black lab chasing waves has her first taste of salt water.
I pull from the rye and collect fuel.

Drive all day for the moment,
standing on a frigid beach
and look at crushing death a few feet away.
The surf is a cold hungry thing.

Tide pounds through sideways cat eye
stone arch to the north.
South the ocean is carving a cave.
The cliff turns into unknown. We remain at the cave.

There have been too many neck deeps,
unseen currents, slick rock, surprise surge,
for us to scramble again.
When the Pacific teaches, you learn.

Runoff dripping purple, gold and red
down the trail and across the beach.
The dog has no interest in this water.
Soon everyone will leave.

My childhood beaches banned fire.
Combustion that requires making up for.
I construct the fire on the tide line.
My goal is to burn the ocean not the forest.

With starlight and fire crackle
sobering travelers must prepare departure.
Delicately removing burning wood from the fire.
Monolith the flames across the beach.

I was born on fire looking beyond the shore.
This moment is my infancy. This beach
is chapel. I fill it with my own image.
I describe to it what it is.

Named Grip

A thing that was assumed.
I arrived and was handed it.
I was told,
"spread it son,
you are built to spread it."

I tried once.
I once saw myself
war.
I was and always
beat myself.

I tell a poison survivor tale.
We tame ourselves with snakes.
See for yourself-
I am always sleeping beauty.
Promised to eat foul. Dead in work.

As I sigh "I"
the front is understood.
I am not an unhinged Patton.
Feel these ruthless paws.
There is only strike.
Welcome to a world of enemy!

I was handed this thing
on the frontlines
of a war unknown.
Wrapped in a pink blanket

and to this day
my girlness unknown.

What I am is a walk away.
What has happened is retreat.
I can only use the weapons I believe in.
I have no strategy.
A lonely private
charged to lead a war.

An explainable-
there were horses,
we knew horses.
There were waters,
spring or river
we were them.

But there are also secret names.
The names that our matriarchy
had to place in reed baskets
and hope for benevolence.
I don't want to hide them
but one of my crests
is a secretkeeper. I have not met the mark.

A forgotten crest-
a rolled scroll,
a flash of foot.
I am out of my family line.
My mouth that never shuts,
my march fist trouble face.
In these ways my name is taken.

I spend my days
working on excommunication
and confirmation.
I work to rebuild a name
and sign off on a rebuttal of name.
What would this familial holding be,
for me, without refusal?

There is a complicated word
that a number of people
are associated with.
We are always mispronounced.
We always say fine.
The snort of nostril is sometimes seen.

So spring never lasts.
Steady yourself.
So the steep slides
and mud is all that is seen.
Sorry, none of us were ready
but this is the line.

Put the name in the secret places.
I had cutting boxes
filled with my favorite scripture verses.
Pain remains pain-
even cleverboxes can't hide.

This thing that came over water.
Traveling like a westward wind.
This badge that doesn't know
what it is made of or why.
It arose and was never born.

We've been out swatting unwanted names.
We've been giving ourselves away
And begging the mystery.
There is no acceptable answer.
A fire always punching up.

I once gave my unknown
and have now been asked to take it back.
I absorb this shadow back into myself.

There is a new crest forming in me.
I am of the house of myself.
People leave their private messages
on my door. I am to read
aloud from the porch.
I am the keeper of disappointment.

I look to those
that carry my same
And how differently we wear it.

I watch friends
dress themselves in their own letters.
I see how dear
the meaning of the line for them.

Once upon a time
I saw myself a soldier
in a different war
and picked another name.
I fled back to my home country.

Though Mars is far away
I believe in it. Not only
in name. I've watched it.
The power of word
is not from the namer.

I've known them as arms
but they might was well
be called sheep or balloon.
They still do what they do.

At times I have lost all names.
Everything is the book of Jeremiah.
Eagles eating eagles that are themselves.
I bled into everything with no discernible borders.

I empty my brush of hair
and don't call it Jeremy.
I have had pieces of my body
cut and disposed of
and never questioned the whereabouts.

I leave my skin everywhere.
There are miles of my body.
Still everything is its own name
and I am fine with this.

My hands are hands
due to them doing what they do.
They close and then
let go so easily.

www.ingramcontent.com/pod-product-compliance
Lightning Source LLC
LaVergne TN
LVHW051457170726
843492LV00002B/707